73

The Feather Room
a collection of poetry

ᚢᚱ

by Anis Mojgani

Write Bloody Publishing
America's Independent Press

Long Beach, CA

writebloody.com

Mojgani, Anis.
1ˢᵗ edition.
ISBN: 978-1-935904-74-8

Interior Layout by Lea C. Deschenes
Cover Designed by Joshua Grieve
Author Photo by Jeremy Okai Davis
Cover Illustration and Interior Illustrations by Anis Mojgani
Proofread by Sarah Kay
Edited by Derrick Brown, Courtney Olsen, Alexis Davis, Jake Danna and Gabrielle Dunkley
Type set in Helvetica by Linotype, Aller and Bergamo: www.theleagueofmoveabletype.com

Also by Anis Mojgani: *Over the Anvil We Stretch*

Special thanks to Lightning Bolt Donor, Weston Renoud

Write Bloody Publishing
Long Beach, CA
Support Independent Presses
writebloody.com

To contact the author, send an email to writebloody@gmail.com

If there is a room inside of me
with your name written in it
the language it is written in is a lovely one.

One of figs and birds
and beaches the color of butter.
The walls blue, and at least one of them
made from nothing but windows
Another has shelves of speckled stones.
The light pours across the floors
and the trees outside
burn with song.

 **THE FEATHER ROOM**

for whom I met inside there

A young man traveling came upon a farm in the night time and stopped to see if he could stay the evening. The farmer that lived there welcomed him in and the young man saw that there were three doors in the living room: a yellow one of wood, a red one of stone, and the third made of blue glass. The farmer said yes the man could sleep on the couch but no matter what he might hear, the man would not open any of the three doors. The young man agreed and lay down to sleep. In the middle of the night he woke to some sound coming from behind the first door. Forgetting the farmer's warning the young man opened the door. Sitting amongst piles of bicycle parts was a beautiful young girl singing and polishing a pair of handlebars. She looked up and motioned for him to join her. He began to polish her arms and immediately he fell asleep. The young man woke to the farmer shaking him and asked the farmer what had happened to the girl. The farmer said that whatever was in that room was now gone and as punishment the young man would have to help him on the farm for the day.

That night the farmer again gave the young man the couch to sleep on and again warned him against opening the doors. Once more the young man was awakened in the night by a sound. He opened up the door of red stone and saw a room filled with birds screeching, every one of them featherless. At the far wall was an old man crying, opening a window. The old man kept picking the birds up and setting them on the sill, as if pushing the creatures out to fly. But all they did was sit there while the old man wept. The young man walked to the old man, who put a featherless bird in the young man's hand and immediately the young man fell asleep. He woke again to the farmer shaking him. He asked what had happened to all the birds and to the old man. The farmer said that whatever was in that room was now gone, and that the young man would have to once more help him on the farm.

That night the farmer again warned the man. And again the young man awoke in the middle of the night. This time though there was only silence. The young man stood in front of the door of blue glass. It was like water except nothing could be seen through it. The silence in the air was so heavy the door seemed to throb. As if all that was silent was on the other side of it. The young man again could not resist and opened the door to walk through. In the morning when the farmer woke him on the floor of the third room he asked the farmer, "What are these rooms?" The farmer looked at him and said, "The first room is the room of where you were, the girl singing was someone you once loved. The second room is the room of where you are, the old man was your sadness holding on to something long gone and broke. And the third room is where you are going. What did you see in there?"

The young man said, "Feathers. There was nothing in the room but feathers."

THE FEATHER ROOM

*We named our children Sweetbelly and Stickylove
and when they were outside, we kept them in fruit trees
and when they were inside we kept them in our arms.*
—A. Davis

Some destinations are moving away while some are approaching.
—Gamma

THE BICYCLE ROOM

The man in the woods
holds his arms out like handlebars
and imagines someone riding him
like a bicycle
—some pretty girl
who could use her long hair to turn him magically.
She would shine him every day after school.
In the sunlight
he would look so pretty
turning in her hands.

ONE SATURDAY AFTERNOON BEFORE I WAS BORN

I was building telescopes from Billy the Kid magazines.

There was an issue where Colonel Dudley had Billy and the Regulators trapped in a house and Dudley had his men set the house on fire. Damn that Colonel. But Billy the big bad water tower that he was broke out of there, escaped. The gang headed for the hills, crossed the mountains in one night, the stars like white animals too far to tell what they were. Billy and the boys hid out in Telegraph Cave. McSween was shot up pretty bad and asked Big Jim French to shoot him. What could Big Jim do? The two of them were like brothers. He went outside so no one would see him cry. They had to head on though before they could bury McSween proper-like, only had time to pile stones over his body. It was real sad-like.

At the back of the pages was an ad for building your own telescope. It said how you could order it and put it together and when you did you could look up into the sky and see the stars real close-up and could make out all the constellations and they had a list of the constellations like Draco the dragon and Scorpius which is a scorpion. No constellation of Billy the Kid or any other cowboys but they had one called Orion who I found out was a warrior that killed Scorpius. I thought how much I would like to see some of those stars closer up. I'd been saving up my money for the past few months to get a real honest to God air rifle like the Watkin Brothers but I thought I might like that there telescope more so I cut out the ad and sent all my money in with it.

I think they sent me the wrong kit.

The instructions were for a short-wave radio. At least that's what it looked like in the picture. I made it anyway. When it was done, I took it into the field past the house. It was Friday night. No one was around. I turned on the radio. There was only static. Across the whole dial, nothing but static. I wondered if it was broken. I wondered if I had put it together wrong. Then a quiet voice, a man's voice sounding real country-like, something like my Pops would listen to, came out through the static. It was still too fuzzy to make out what the words were but I kinda liked it. The sky was so blue and dark it was like the inside of a magician's hat and everything had spilled out. I sat there in the high grass and listened to that nameless country singer singing something I couldn't understand. Them stars were real close.

1

Such birds, such GREAT BIRDS
sit in the sky of your neck.
When close to me,
as you sleep as you move—
how I watch them.

THE FEATHERS

1.
I was born with them in my arms.
Would stay up at night plucking them all out, didn't want the other kids to see them. Back when I was four I was in the yard and some boys from down the street saw me.
Hey bird.
You! Bird boy!
You chicken? You taste like chicken?
I like my chicken fried.

They tried to cook me. I have a crooked ear from the flames.
Ever since, I always pluck them out. Every few nights they grow back. And I pluck again.

2.
From the darkness outside I hear the geese in the field. I watch for them in the sky, balancing the moon on their backs. On clear nights the world above me looks like an ocean, an upside-down bowl of blackness spilling onto all of us, ready to cave in. I listen for the hiss of the stars, the sound of their gas escaping, waiting for their deflated skin to fall to the earth.

3.
After the plucking my arms are always covered in little red bumps. My mother is starting to look at me strangely—my father always has. I think Mom thought that one day they would stop growing, that one day they would just be gone. Every birthday of mine her eyes dim a little more with each approaching realization: perhaps her son is a mistake, perhaps God used her body to cough a boy out.

4.

I collect them in a crate in my closet. They are heavier than one might think. Yes, they're light enough to make the bird mock gravity. But when so many of them weave their waves over the arms the body begins to drag, the bones begin to heavy. When my skin is barren of them, I can feel every part of the wind pushing through every part of me. When they grow back full I can't sleep. I move about and feel like I'm moving through water.

5.

When the crate is full I empty it into a large bag that I keep hidden in the shed. There is an abandoned airstrip behind the house—when the bag is full I go there and make a small mountain from the bag's contents. I light the pile. I wait for the plume of smoke to fill the whole sky. It colors the clouds with the blackness of the burning. But there is never enough smoke. The feathers become ash. When I head back home with the bag, I leave the ash behind.

6.

One night the geese stop talking. I strain to listen. I hear the hissing stars. I stare out the window and see a light in the atmosphere darken and fall, flying to the earth like a bleeding balloon. Leaping from bed I run to the air strip. Upon the ground I find what looks like a dead white cat stitched from light. The star breathes brokenly, its chest rising and falling. I pick it up and start rubbing it over my arms— wringing drops of it onto my shoulders, kneading the drops into the skin, hoping to kill all this that grows out of my limbs, wishing the things I pull out of me I'll lose, finally washed free of this heavy coat, and come morning my body will be smooth.

SUNSET PARK

New York City is a feather beneath his pillow.
That was the year he learned to live under a sunset.
Stuck between the faceless warehouses of south Brooklyn,
he filled sheets of big paper with orange birds.
It was the year he distanced himself from the trains
yelling into Manhattan. Traded in sleep for a 4 track recorder.
The machine taught him to slow down the guitar scream.
He made storms on the Korg.
Looking up at the buildings gave him vertigo in reverse.
He wanted to claw into the heavens. Hip-hop gave him the same feeling.
So did the curve of her lip. The arching of her back. The bread he broke
alone at dawn. In an empty apartment she wilted against him.
He gave away his virginity that year. Like a sack of gold
dropped in a river of snakes and light, he thought
The cops'll never find it here.
He made a marker in the sand to find his way back
to this place on the bank. But a current is too strong
to keep anything too long.
That was the year the subway painted itself inside of him.
Falling asleep to its lullaby, his chin against his chest,
blossoms squeezed out his shut eyes.
His dreams pushed into his shoulders
sleep replaced by the clang of iron and steel.
This is where both dreams and love come from—
the clang of iron and steel.
Swallowing the city after work. Waking in the dark
to catch the train on time. Pulling clothes on like a whisper
with no one to tell it to. Trying to listen to himself. Trying to ford that river.
But March is a long month. It is born of hunger.
And does not break quickly.
Sometimes it stretches through the following winters.

He fell in love twice that year, all the flowers in the South.
Held tight two horses galloping in opposite directions. Found himself
on the ground. The dust, the burn. The sky, a shined pair of boots.
He wore the heels through. Kept wearing them.
Hung his shoes over the lamp.
The night held pearl necklaces by the fistful—sometimes a tease,
sometimes the exhaling of a perfect shape. He wrote poems
about what this told him. His chest filled
with a heavy lump of mineral
that pulled at the metal of the sky.

BEEHIVE/ LODESTONE

All that has touched me is carried inside a swarm of bees.
One day that swarm of bees will carry me to heaven.
This is why the compass and our bodies
both swing north.

PHOTOSYNTHESIS

There are so many flowers in my mouth!
Growing!
What gardeners your kisses are! *Gardeners! PARADING!*
All over my skin!
I am dark rich and bounteous earth
sloped for walking through and you parade
all about this land.
Such things you leave inside of me!
Such bulbs
that grow
and move in the movement of sun.
Such seeds that the sunlight races
to find my skeleton and join its bones,
fighting to get in here,
fighting to push inside and fill me, causing
all these flowers in my mouth to burst forth.

AT EIGHT

the hummingbirds buried themselves in my belly my eyes swallowed
up the evening a swarm in the hazy sunlight of dusk buzzing silently
bringing the bones of their beaks out the bushes in the backyard
our house was made of wood but stood on bricks standing on the
back steps I saw myths or gods childhood or all three taking shape
together from the green feathers carving figure eights inside the
sunset a million wing beats the blood kept rushing from knees to feet
to skull like a secret I stood on the stairs too fragile to move screen
door held open by little fingers all but my heart had forgotten how
to breathe I was water turned solid the sun on the other side of the
trees undressed itself brightly into the approaching night its flocks of
fingers beckoned

THE GIANT GOLDEN BOY OF BIOLOGY

1.
I am in the desert building poems.
They look like mobiles and taste of jet fuel.
This great expanse of rock and star
is the only place that can fit me.
Sitting atop the plateaus at night,
high above the earth, the flat rock
the only place bigger than my hands,
I wrap myself in the large sheet of the sky
to better examine the molecules
moving through my body.

2.
Hard to believe how small I once was.
That there was another person I came out from.
That my mother carried me inside her body.
I came from something,
from a certain size,
just like everyone else.
Except I kept growing.
Mother says she still loves me,
that she can still fit me in her heart
even if not her arms.

3.
There are many stories about me—
how I use pine trees as back scratchers
and rivers for cups.
Stories of how my footprints make canyons,
how the ground beneath me rumbles when I snore.

Of how my skin has so much shine,
the full moon becomes a quiet goose.
If a cloud of birds flies past my mouth as I sleep
I sometimes accidentally breathe them in.
There are flocks building castles inside my body.

4.
One night on the plateau I shouted my stories.
Held them like sharp dirt and bled.
I watched the blood make a lake
and made a boat to place in the lake.
I sailed it.
The boat and I were theatre.
I sailed it.
The lions came out to watch.
I set the boat on fire for them to learn what this body can do.
They clapped. They roared.
They asked if I needed a ride.
This was real.
I sat on the back of one.
He roared and raced like the wind.
I felt a greater wind move against me.
The lion's back was gold fur.
So soft. I believed my mother loved me as much as I know she does.
The inside of her is a planet made up of smaller planets.
The inside of her is a kingdom made up of smaller kingdoms.
Her children are all her kings.
Her kings are made of smaller kings—
our bodies are kingly bodies
made up of billions of other kingly possibilities.
My nephew is her smallest greatest king of us all.
He is a star burning in a paint can.
I cannot put a lid on my love.
All I can do is take these giant arms of mine like tree trunks
dip them into that star,

and like paintbrushes
swing them
across empty spaces
to see what falls through the clouds.

ELIZABETH PART II

She took me to that city on the coast.
The one in North Carolina that she lived in
with the boy she knew before me.
Years later she brought me there,
to the car she once slept in and hadn't seen since.
She showed me the boat his father had been building for years.
The car and boat were in the same field.
We opened the trunk and went through the back seat.
It was filled with things she had left behind, faded and bent
from being washed in the sunlight.
When we drove off we took with us her pair of black boots
and some of the records that hadn't warped.
She took me to the gazebo by the water,
to the small brick home on the edge of the swamp
closed up and empty now.
She pointed out the large house they squatted in, tall and eaten by vines.
The car made marks in the wet mud as we turned it around.
We drove down the road so she could take me to her favorite spot
but when we got to the turn off where the dirt turns red,
there were dozer treads in it from turning the dirt over.
There were men in bright hats
standing around pick-up trucks, rifles in hand.
We thought of accidentally being shot in the woods and turned back.
We walked past the library instead,
got ice cream.
There were bricks in the ground
and moss growing on the ones in the shade.
The sun filled everything with emptiness.
We walked to the docks
and leaned on the railing.
The water below us

moved of its own accord.
Without me learning what was in those woods
we headed back west.

I WAS IN A HOUSE ON FIRE

I was in a house on fire. It was surrounded. The soldiers surrounding it were all on horses. They had made a ring around the building. The soldiers pulled out swords and trumpets. They flashed one and blew into the other. I stayed inside. I had set the fire. Those men were not going to take me alive, or at all. I climbed into the basement, pulled the door shut behind me. I would be safe down here. I had built a lock that was indestructible. I had everything I needed: grains and grass, a small orange tree. Even had a box with a piece of the sky in it. I had found it behind the farm many years ago. It wasn't much to look at. Had obviously been cast aside due to its sickly nature. But I had taken it in and nursed it, and it had grown somewhat. I didn't need much else. I could stay down here as long as I needed to.

I did.
I stayed in the basement for 317 years.

One day I climbed up my steps and opened the door. In the time that had passed, a large department store of the future had been built over the place where I had once set fire to my house. I tried to buy some new clothes but the only thing they sold were flowers.

THE ICEBERG ROOM

The room held an iceberg.
They had trapped it together.
On hot days the iceberg melted in spots
leaving puddles on the floor.
Poor and shirtless they collected the water
and drank it. Their veins widened
and their hearts were able to push more blood faster.
Iceberg flowed inside them.
This is how their children will become part glacier.
And why on a family trip to Patagonia
he will lead them across the snows, tell them
to put their ears to the ice beneath their feet.
Listen, he will say.
This is what your grandfathers kept building
and taking apart. Finally they gave up.
Realized it wasn't going anywhere.
And perhaps it was better that way.
When all of them stand up, they will brush the snow from their legs
and watch the sun pour itself across the South American sky.
The colors entering the glacial wall will split it with a song.
They, being part glacier,
will all feel a burning in their lungs.

WONT YOU COME OUT TONIGHT?

At the top of the hill is a small but very tall house.
The boys in town go there
to try and knock out the highest windows.
They do this to impress the girls they drag up there with them.
The girls smile and whisper
while the boys pretend to fight.
The boys believe the louder their body is the brighter their hearts will look
—they push each other and jump into the air.
They make fists. They play-fight,
and imagine what it means to not be scared.
The girls laugh at this because they imagine the same thing
but in a different way. The girls do this to hide
the quiet libraries of curiosity they hold in their chests.
They pretend to know how the world works,
that the boys are silly and know too much about nothing.
The girls pick up rocks to show how one throws something with weight.
The boys shrug this off.
They are not impressed or pretend not to be.
But the book on the inside of their skin is bound
of the same trembling papers the girls are made of.

Neither of them yet know
what the shapeless water of love is,
anything they hold tightly falls between their fingers.
They are wet. But their hearts
have begun to quicken.
And run six footed.
And dance
around the fire.
And in certain hours of touching
feel sparks flying out of them.

They watch and whisper. The few times they hear the distant breaking
of glass from up on high, little trees inside their chests uproot themselves
and become small but very tall houses with brand new windows
placed in their walls waiting for the world to break its way inside.

This is why they come to the house—
to show how far their bodies can send something into time.
To show how far into the dark they can hurl the earth.
To make sing some small rock pitched perfect on accident.

WHAT SHE SAID

HER: When you see your self, tell him I don't know anything about what's going to happen but tell him that when I saw him I thought: *I am going to be his wife.* That I know.

HIM: When you see *your* self, tell her that *my* self doesn't know anything either but when he saw you he knew the same thing.

BEFORE THE CHERRY FESTIVAL

We returned to the lake,
to a house filled with lights and poets,
and escaped out the back doors
to the nape of the beach.
We walked to the end of a broken pier
and sat in the wind.
How bright the dark lake was.
Under the fullness of the stars
every translucent part of me gained clarity.
You were no stranger to wanting your heart
to be anything but a muscle you called your own.
But earlier in the evening you told me
you knew you were going to marry me.
We stared above us.
In the morning we woke before everyone else,
made a plate of fruit and danishes
and ate it outside.
I spun you on a merry-go-round of metal.
There was no danger in watching you smile.
Only a blur of color. The sunlight,
not needing to fight its way into our bodies,
no need for it to even curl its fist,
was welcomed happily by both of us.
You wore my sweater,
the one with the red horse on the left breast.
All that you are came into me.
My body for so long had been a bag of holes.
You took matchsticks,
turned them into architecture.

SATURDAY

Outside
the sun on me.
Eating my breakfast.
My strawberries.
My cereal.
This is how easy the world can work.
The thought of your arms near—
so close I could hear them.
This is how easy the world can work.

THE GENERAL & HIS LOVER

How her clothes come off and go back on is a miracle—it is magic.
Her skin a pack of wet colts parading as musicians. All her muscle
is music making. I watch all of this. Her spit moves through my
body, while a revolution continues outside. Mother—out there
they are calling for my head. O Mother, how did I end up here?
The summers amongst the trees watching you pick the fruits for the
Baron, I never thought I would end up here, with her spit moving
through my body, the sword of a dead general tied at my waist.
Dressed in only the cloth of the afternoon we moved over each other
like animals, sunlight curling under the drawn shade, clawing across
our shoulders. The days leave scars.

What brought me to this place, Mother?
I fucked this woman because I love her Mother. Because I love the
taste of her legs, the taste of her chest in my mouth—how its heart
beats upon my tongue, against my teeth. Her sweat is a strong tea.
I lick between her legs trying to escape.

This room creaks like a sleeping man. My boots polished and cast
to the floor. The general's sword lies next to them. What ship
brought me here Mother? After I killed the general I took the
sword I killed him with and rather than give it to anyone I threw it
in the river. Perhaps it is still in that mud, rusted and stuck. I can't
remember to which bend in the river I flung the saber. Someplace
close to our village Mother. Someplace close to where Brother and I
ate those peaches we stole.

Mother. The woman I love is a jaguar. I could watch her clothes go on
and go off and back on over and over again. The way her hips disappear
into the waist of her dress and become something just as magical as
when naked. How her legs and back dissolve into the folds of clothing,
how I know what is under there—those secrets between us moving

like a game children play with trees. The people outside yell for my skin. They wish to drape it over their bodies. To wave it from a flagpole. To carry their dead cattle inside of it. To lay it across the bones of their buried uncles.

My heart sighs. They have already sent cannonballs flying into my walls. Some wing of this manor has crumpled. My lover is buttoning her blouse. She looks up and smiles. I get up, dressed only in what you and Father gave me, and stop her. I start unbuttoning the blouse, pulling her breasts, her waist, out from the rustling fabric. I take the blade I took from the dead man and tie it back around me. All I want is to fuck her again. While all around me is crumbling. The hills outside are painted in gold.
They look like her chest moving into mine.

SOUTHWEST OF THE RIVER

There was a window in the bedroom.
Her bed was beneath it. In the afternoon and with the lamp off
we stretched on the mattress.
Sometimes touching each other, sometimes not.
Sometimes our fingers just lingered,
the day lying across us and the walls,
the color of the walls mixing
with the sun's dead empty light.
It made everything in the room white.
Soft. Open.
That's what I remember.

SCOUT

In the night trees outside
a mockingbird's talking.
I don't know how far away
whoever he's talking to is,
but I'm here
listening, and one car
drives down the empty street,
and just now
another one.

PAUSING IN DOORWAYS TO STAND

He's been shutting doors more softly
trying to notice how lovely
some of the doorknobs
fit in his hand.
She sits in the doorway.
There are tiny pale blue flowers
that grow all over her body.
Her flowers watch the world.
Their petals stitched of fabric
and sewn of a dress she is wearing.

He sits close to her
whispering quietly.
And so quietly
he
can't even make out
what he wants to say.
He doesn't even know
if his lips
are moving.
His body clicks like a silent movie.
When she leaves the room for a moment
he steals some of her perfume
on his wrist.

THE NAILS

Under the moonlight he digs them up—
prostrating in the soil,
swallowing the broken nails down.
This is what he has lived off of for so long—
he must feed the birds something.

Licking the place where the shadows have been,
trying to taste the dance taken in those spots,
he no longer knows how to use his teeth.
His body stands on many legs,
his house built from many songs
with many rooms nailed out of its insides.
So many windows in them—
faces peek in, the songs leak out.
The sky fills with many balloons.
His hands fill with strings
and with an insatiable hope
to replace skin with love.
Hope however sometimes becomes curiosity.
He never wanted to replace the love with the skin
but the telephone poles do not speak as loudly as they once did.
No longer knowing how to talk back
he wakes in the middle of the night sweating,
still able to hear the music
from those many rooms of far away,
and crawls outside
to dig the dark land up with his hands.

FROM COLLECTING BUTTONS

Dark flowers becoming bright stones.
A tree stump moving in reverse.
A piano outside.
Spitting the rain back into the sky's saucepan.
A juggler washing his face.
A fridge filled with 10 jars of water waiting to pour.
The buttons still on a coat.

ISLANDS

Holding the gentle storm of my head inside this gentle body of paper
I float
just above the surface of the floor.
At this low of an altitude
the heart hums.
Like a coin trying to spin
but stuck standing.

One side wished
for the two of us to sail backwards,
to meet again
in the middle of those seas,
arriving together on an island of turquoise.
The other wish
was to find my way back
to an island of open orchards,
where the apples are heavy and cover the ground.
The fruit there causes one to forget.
An island where the monsters cut off all their hair,
and the boys, lying all day in the pastures,
learn how to become golden again.

IN THE FIELD

Shoot it through the bottle. Like, through the opening of the bottle.

This is what the man tells the boy.
The boy is confused. Sometimes the stars
make electronic noises. They speak like computers.
The boy does not tell anyone else this. He is standing
in the middle of the field. And the man with the blue jeans
is telling him to shoot the gun. *Aim for the hole* in the bottle.
The boy thinks sometimes there must be a tray inside his hands
and the tray is made of some heavy metal. But he can carry it.
Sometimes there are piles of things on it. Flanks of meat
dripping with weight. His arms get tired.
He wants to come in from the storms. But he's been told
if he stands in the rain with the dead things in his arms
something may happen. The man in the blue jeans
didn't tell him this. But someone did.
He can't remember their face. He forgets the faces often.
The circuitry in the sky beepboops too loud. The red lights in the heavens
push his dreams out of his head. In the morning he finds himself
on his knees. Scraping his floor for whatever fallen pieces there may be.
He has no place to put them. Only the tray. And that tray—
that thing of flat heavy metal—
it is so sticky with blood.

WHAT HIS MOTHER SAID

"Once my hands were made of milk.
I took a lover under the boughs of my father's trees.
He drank from my eyes.
They were like little spoons holding little hills of sugar.
His heart was a hive of bees that did not buzz.
All my friends were imaginary and had different hair lengths.
All the flowers bent towards my ankles when I walked.
There was more than one sun then.
The sun that shone on Tuesday
was not the same one that shone on Sunday.
Tuesday's was skinny and silent—she wore a long dress.
Wednesday's was always changing her name.
Friday's was always asleep behind the garden,
his belly fat with tomatoes.
Saturday's could fit in my pocket.
Sunday's was made of ice but was always sweating.
On Sunday evening Mother would draw the bath,
and I would sit in the water with the window open.
One night a man with a bag came through it,
put me in the bag and took me away on a horse.
I counted the steps his steed took.
It stopped on the 3045th.
The man held me in his arms and carried me somewhere.
It was a small house.
The man told me he took me to take as his wife.
He gave me a dress and my own room and tied the horse up.
There was a river chained up out back.
I could hear it cry when I slept.
Sometimes the river talked but nothing was there.
I wondered if the river was crazy.

Time passed. I could no longer remember
if Monday's sun smelled of onions or tea.
Thursday was the only sun that came around me anymore.
She buried wildflowers and trembled in the wind.
She could whistle with her front teeth.
One day I watched her
make all the silverware stand straight up on their own.
I took to going barefoot through the rooms and the woods.
The man sometimes forgot to feed the river.
It had grown skinny and snapped its teeth if you walked too close.
At night I would hear it scratch itself.
I lay awake by the window,
thought about braiding hair I couldn't see.
I became a pitcher.
The man would hold me and drink my fingers out of me.
They were cool and so white.
I watched him wipe their cream from his lips with the back of his hand."

RAZI'S LEMON TREE

My beautiful lemon tree I grew from a seed.
How big you have gotten!
You were so little when you were a seed.
Now, so big. And soon
you will carry such round
and lovely lemons,
yellow
and dimpled.
When they are too big for your thin branches
and they leave this kitchen of mine,
ask them not to forget it—this kitchen of ours.
It is my favorite room in the house.
And lemon tree
when you pick up
to follow,
please do think of me.
I will think of you.
Here, when my tongue
is far too sweet,
and my hands far too empty
I will think
of the quiet poem of your shape.
Lemon tree,
please bring a scarf with you.
Wherever you end up may be cold.
And if it isn't, perhaps
you will vacation someplace where it is.

AND A STACK OF PLATES FOR COMPANY

The house cats yawn and step outside.
The roof has holes but it barely rains.
I have a collection of barrels for when it does.
The bathtub has clawed feet
like the one we had growing up.
Inside it is one of my dining room tables.
There is a candlestick holder in its center.
This is alright.
I rarely take a bath.
Should I want to, I have the collection of barrels.
In the green beetle grass of the yard
it is always night
when it is night.
And always daylight when it is daytime.
The dirt is filled with silverware.
From me throwing them upwards.
Towards the stars.
I throw them up in code
sending the stars messages.
The clouds get to them first
and send them back with messages of their own.
The yard is littered with words and soup spoons.
Under the moon the sentences brightly gleam.
This is also where I place the good china.
In case there is ever company
I pull out the best plates
and prepare the bathtub for guests.
It is also where I sleep.
Under the table.
I have a pillow for you.
When you land here, tell me.

2

there are bees in my heart
bees in my chest
bees in my mouth
flying out
flying out
flying out

DICTION

The people in town seemed surprised. Like they had never seen a flock of bees come out of someone's mouth before. It wasn't even so much the bees. Or the wasps. Or the tiny tiny rainstorms. It wasn't the shining rings or the swans of amber that any of them seemed to be surprised by. It wasn't even my mouth. They told me: *It's just, that's not how we talk.*

I said something back. Some…some word. I don't know if it was an emerald or a tugboat or some yellow yellow petal. But after it fell I turned to walk back through the scarves, leaving footprints in the flowers, hoping someone would use them to follow me home. Afraid of whom it might be, somebody who knew what I was trying to say.

FROM UNDER THOSE SILVER BLANKETS

When they went out to find me, if they had looked properly,
they would have found me in the fields with the cows,
before the sun came up, while the sky was still filled with fog
and the fog was dropping his feet softly, sneaking lightly across the hills,
wet toes quietly touching down. He came like a silver god from a grey
hole, shaking out the color from his blue shoulders—he joined us there.
If they had looked properly they would have found me out there with him.
Being kissed by the morning when it still had sleep in its eyes.
Praying with the cows in a broken circle: knees bent, mouths
full of grass, the dew o so sweet. The only sound was our hearts
chewing. I wasn't wearing shoes, I didn't even have on my shirt.
Only a stain smeared cross my chest, from where I had wiped the dirt
off my hands to better taste the earth.

LONG AFTER JANUARY HAD PASSED

From the side of the highway I notice
how the rain this winter
has pulled so much
out of the Texas wildflowers.
They bleed so many colors.

IT IS MAY

There are some seconds that still stick sometimes,
stuck
still wondering
why you never came back
and why I spent so long
thinking you might.
There are scratches in all records,
we are built to now and then click through time.

Five minutes after this
my arms bend like a worshipping mantis.
I get up from the dinner table to add that line.

6 minutes before
there is opera thundering out of a computer.
Outside is Texas in the springtime.
The earth is swallowing rain—
to grow out of the soil
I am moving backwards through the dirt.
Tonight I will use the bicycle
to bleed myself out of me,
to fall back into the field of yellow petals
my body has been becoming.

HER YELLOW ROOM

There were birds trapped in that yellow room.
You kept bringing them home.
Look at this one you'd say. *His ankle is sprained.*
It looks fine to me, I'd say, and turn back to my book.
But you kept bringing them home.

Lying together in bed, we had to make room for them all.
This one had feathers missing. This one's feathers were coated
in something sticky. This one had a strange shake when it walked.
I never saw anything wrong with any of them.
But still they kept on being brought inside.
All shapes sizes and colors, flapping round the room.
Feathers everywhere. Shrieking and squawking.
Dishes of seed spilled all across the carpet.
I tried to read.

With so many birds it began to smell like the zoo.
With so many birds fights would break out. They'd peck
at each other, pull at the wings, pull blood. Some nights
you could calm them. You would start to sing, quietly cooing.
Whatever they were all screaming about and clawing at would cease.
They would soften. Stay still. You sat on the floor telling them a story.
I would put my book down, listen with them, their heads gently
bobbing like the ocean. Like them, I felt coated in feathers
as white as the first ones. I was so soft.
The room was so soft.

Time passed though and there became too many of them.
You had to start taking things out to make space for the birds.
First little things. The lamp. The television. Dishes from the floor.
The record player and its records. Then the furniture started going.

The night stand. The orange chair from the corner. The chest of drawers.
You stacked your books into towers and threw out the bookshelves
but eventually the books went as well. The birds started eating them.
The books I had given you were cut up to make nests. Some books
you hid under the carpet but the birds found them. We got rid of the bed,
the sheets, the pillows, and slept on the floor. They slept in your socks.
They got into everything. They got ill. Started coughing, their feathers
falling to their feet. They shed their skin. Became bald and quiet.
You would stay up with droppers of medicine. It smelled like sickness.

I would try to sleep, but I couldn't. When I did, I dreamed of you singing.
All I wanted was to sleep and hear this. I would wake and ask for you
to sing to me but you couldn't. You had given too much to the birds—
your voice, the notes you held in your breast. I watched how quiet
the world in that room became. It felt like a town that had emptied of all
but us and we hoped that wasn't the case. Or perhaps we were the town
and the room was a pair of bodies silently moving through us.

I stayed inside it until the feathers pushed me out the door. The last I saw
of you, you were kneeling in a carpet of them. It looked like snow
had fallen in your bedroom. You were holding as many birds
as you could in a tight embrace, your arms full of wings and beaks.
You were on your knees singing silently into their staring bodies,
their heads bobbing like they were still coated in white white feathers.
I curled my fingers around my shoulders and walked off backwards,
my head nodding like theirs.

ICEBERG HUNTING

The iceberg puts up a beautiful fight
—O how it gnashes its teeth.
Should you get bitten by one
lilies bloom,
sometimes chrysanthemums,
from the gash.
They are red as cherries.
They bloom from your blood
until the wound like a garden
looks up at you.
You watch the petals grow and wilt
and fall.
And more grow in their place.
Until the growing grows faster than the falling.
And the holes in your skin
begin pushing out too many flowers to keep up with.
These flowers the last thing you see.
Even when you die
all you will think of
is their shape and color
scarring your body
like a field of red flowers
blooming through
the blue hands of the Arctic.

WHEN ONE BODY GOES & ANOTHER APPEARS THIS IS WHAT THE BOYS ARE LEFT WITH, THIS IS HOW THEY MUST MOVE WHAT IS IN THEM

The boy sits holding a glass of water. The glass of water is his. His hands are still as cold teapots in the snow. The water is assuredly still. Holding it is what saves him. Inside he trembles.

There are two more glasses on the table before him. One is full. The other is empty. The rains have always brought the water, he never asks where they bring it from. He just holds tight.

The gods play pinball with his heart some days. And some days they play darts. There are tiny holes in the walls. In his closet the gods sit like feathers inside his shirts.

The boy's job is to take the glass in his hand, and transfer the water into the empty glass on the table. He must also fill the glass he is already holding with the water from the third glass. And though the two glasses on the table are smaller than the one in his hands he must somehow fill the glasses to capacity. The pouring between the glasses must all be done at the same time. The water cannot spill. The water cannot mix. These are the rules.

Outside the sun is fighting to come indoors. It has a long filthy tongue and rattles its fists. But the boy has been practicing his scary face on the brooms in the corner. He will not be scared. He tells himself this and dares physics to come forward.

The sun bangs on the windows. The gods are asleep or somewhere else—tipping over a bucket of milk. Setting a haystack on fire. The boy has two hands and a glass in each.

THE BALLOONIST & THE FLAUTIST

She came upon him in the snow
chopping wood to bring inside.
He looked up at her and stared.
He did not look away.
She handed him a cup.
She put it in his hands like he was a sanctuary.
He put his lips to it like it was a flute
and he didn't know a flute could make music.
She watched him like a small cat.
He watched her like a tired bird.
She could see his breath move.
He stood like a hair
and said:

You can stay
but there are parts of forever dropped into other rivers.
Those stones may take away from the ones I have still to give
—do not expect me to go fishing for these other ones.
Do not expect me to search for and bring them back to you.

He watched her like a scared bird.
She watched his breath moving in front of his mouth.
It was a small swirling cloud.
She made a wish on it.

Inside,
putting the cup back with the others,
she saw his cigarettes on the floor.

He never smoked them.
Only stacked them next to one another
in neat little rows.

THIS TOWN

all the grasses in this town leap

all the birds sing in Inuit accents

the trees dress themselves up like castles

on Halloween the cars all pretend to be horses

and all the ghosts dress like generals

feathers in their hats

swords to the sky

the one rides the other all night long

they bark at the loud planets

and carry torches in their hands

everyone gets a good scare

but we all laugh because it is a good scare

and know that the next day

the ghosts will be in the buttresses of the trees

hanging there

asleep

their sheets blowing in the early morning like toilet paper

thrown by children drunk on time

their bodies like a party all fallen asleep

their feathery hats laying in the grass

like a slipper of champagne filled with dew

THIS HOUSE

Call me a wild thing.
In the house in my body
sometimes there is a creak.
Sometimes the wind. Sometimes the spirits.
Call me a wild thing. There are wildflowers growing
through the porch. It has rained not too long in the past.
You can tell in how green the grass is. How washed the world feels.
The finches nest in the chimney. Its black bricks are cracked.
The cracks are filled with leaves. In the dusk the finches funnel in.
They look like a tornado returning to its start, birthing itself from a storm
back into nothing. Call me a wild thing.
In the dawn the finches flood like ink
into the weakening dark. Their ink bodies spill into the sky.
The sky's black bricks are cracked.
The cracks are filling with dawn. Call me a wild thing. I am
on the porch. Listening to the creaks my weight makes
on the wood. I sniff flowers. Smell earth and blood.
There is something in the woods.
A girl. I can smell her from here.
She is lying in the grass. White dress. Wet.
Heart still moving. Skin pale as flour.

Call me a wild thing. I run sometimes. Sometimes I sleep
beneath the ancient tree. My belly is softer than my back.
There are things inside of me that are overgrown with blackberries.
They are plump with the sun, ready to stain fingers.
There is a room where a woman with a loom weaves.
She is making a fabric, like skin, white as a ghost. The light
passes through it. Her body is like lace.
The light passes through it.
Its corners curl into shapes and beautiful patterns.
She lays herself before me on top of the table

and places my teacup onto her chest.
They are both trembling things.
She covers her body with teacups, balancing,
braces herself for any movement in the earth.
The earth is a trembling thing. I lay at her feet
and kiss her ankle.
We are all trembling things.

ON THE EASTSIDE OF MY BODY

I have a girl that lives in a little silver trailer in Texas. Sometimes
I call her "Love" sometimes I call her "Darling." Sometimes I call her
by her real name. My darling walks around the rooms inside my chest
hanging chandeliers, opening windows. She lets the night in, the crickets
in. She turns the radio on and lets the songs find their way outside to
coat the grass with summertime.

When it rains in Texas it rains hard, and when it rains hard
Lordy how the little trailer feels even smaller. It is made of steel though.
Steel. All of my body is dark rain falling. In the middle of it there is a silver
and steel silver-bullet shaped thing, made of *silver* and *steel*. My body
makes music against it, trying to get inside there. How patient it sits,
waiting for me to do this. How patiently she sits.

MY GHOSTS

My ghosts come correct son.
At quarter to four in the black morn
they come in my house cigarettes hanging,
dragging mud onto the carpet.
They stick their hands in the cold of the fridge,
fingertips dangling over the roast leftovers.
I can hear them swallowing down cold chicken.
When done they put the empty bowls back on the refrigerator shelf.
Cold.
They stay awhile—
mud on the carpet.
Feet kicked up.
Bones on the plate.
The lazy fan in the ceiling spinning
real s l ow.
Them ghosts they napping in the living room.
Heavy like a submarine they lie.
They been eating all day.
They feast on me even when I sleep.

BALLROOM II

Every day I wake surrounded
by my past lovers standing like a choir
of silent angels over me.
Statues in a garden.
Beneath their stares
I get dressed
and through the hours of the day
keep them close,
like a pair of brass knuckles,
stretching my fingers through the holes
cold around my skin,
like the gloves of a knight,
chainmail
pulled up to the elbow to keep me
from touching anything.
Every night I still find myself
holding such heaviness around my fists
unable to unclench the fingers
walking into the lake
its waters coming over my shoulders.

AVIGNON

We sat on stone steps in the south of France
eating gelato under the perfect heat of Avignon.
We stared at the pigeons and in certain moments
I wouldn't wonder if we still loved one another.
Instead walked through the tiny streets
of this walled city in the midst of a theatre festival;
there were posters on every scrap of brick.
We found shade and trees and a canal running green.
You bought a German copy of Madam Bovary for Blaire.
It has a tattered red cover and sits in my garage.
In the grocer's store next to the ice cream shop
we bought delicious fruit,
peaches and plums.
The grocer said we should come back
buy bread and meat and cheese,
picnic on the grass by the water.
We thought *splendid*
and believed we would do so.
Instead we stumbled into my parents,
joined them at an outdoor table
for a dinner too expensive for what it was.
In Avignon there are alleys cobbled in pale marble,
open squares where the light waits for something to do.
And in the golden dusk the locals gather
with skateboards and wine bottles
outside the former pope's castle.
We walked up its stairs,
saw the whole town.
The room we slept in was hot.
We kept the skinny windows open
and one night we crossed to the field outside

where a Ferris wheel large and like a still fire
luminous
was waiting for us.
Somehow I was easily convinced to ride it with you.
It didn't matter how high the wheel spun
my fear was left with the gravity.
It stopped spinning
and we just sat there,
staring into the black black black
blackblack sky
like it was a country to be looked at
and not climbed through.
There was a breeze.
We wore sweaters
but I felt naked.
Every heavy weight my days had piled into my lap
I left.
And being that close to you and so far away,
like a land to be looked upon
and not climbed through,
I felt like I was only just then being made.
Carved from marble,
being polished.

RECIPE

a boat
a bed
a round window
a tree of lemons
a tree of oranges
salted bacon
a ladder tall enough for harvesting
a notebook for clouds
a blanket made from different squares
a dog
a tinier boat on the back of the bigger one
a full bookshelf
my first pocketknife
a bible written of rabbit poetry
a candelabra in tiny pieces to piece back together on moonless nights
and a heart made from the neck of a giraffe
because I want my love to be long
                              long
                              long
                              long

THE MAGICIAN

I can do magic he says.
She doesn't believe him.
I can.
Without touching her, he lifts.
She looks at her feet, a few inches off the floor.
She looks at him, smiles.
He smiles back,
sets her down,
and pulls a rabbit out of her hat.

THE CRAB IN YOUR HAND HAS THE PRETTIEST SPOTS ON ITS CLAWS

Standing in the basin of the rocks, I sweep my arm over the view of their giant shapes and say "All this I make for you. Or at least I try to. Some of it comes out beautiful. The rest, well I try." Off the shore the ocean swells, like wind rippling under a sheet. It keeps coming back to us.

THIS IS WHAT IT IS:

a heart made of marbles
a pocket filled with crumbs of colored paper
a train tunnel painted pink
swallowing a paintbrush
filling the pillowcases with sand
breaking eggs just for the sound
our anvils become flocks of tiny geese
bending ourselves over them
we become water
all the light sits on us

DOWN SOUTH

I had just come out from a yard.
In the yard was a car a woman
and a man most likely about to kill the woman.
I knew this when I left.
I had talked my way out of being killed as well,
convincing him I wouldn't tell anyone.
When I woke I was so ashamed of this.
More than any other thing I've ever dreamed of.
As I rounded the edge of the yard's chain link fence
the last thing I saw
was her on the car's hood,
he was a panther.
I kept walking.

I came into a courtyard,
Ted was getting married
and the bride was from South America.
It was mid afternoon.
There was a tree
and stones set in the ground—
chairs all around
and string lanterns tied up.
The country the bride was from started with a P.
Chris was drunk and talked the whole time.
I was embarrassed.
Ted wouldn't get married.
They left and he broke the girl's heart.
I apologized to her family
and followed to find them.
There was a blue light dangling
off over the horizon,
like a fly on the end of the line.

It looked like one of those fish
with the lamps growing out of their heads,
the lamp's tip.
Three Mexican gentlemen with mustaches
and matching light blue suit jackets
began saying the Lord's Prayer to me.
I took off my hat and started weeping.

THERE ARE ROOTS IN THE GROUND THAT POKE OUT THE EARTH

When the cloak slips and I stumble over my stupid clumsy feet please pull the fabric back over my shoulders.

BEFORE THE DANCE

In the middle of the woods
the hares and the foxes circled me.
Even with myself so heavy and so full of wolf,
heavy and choking on rubies—
even so,
they still came in closer.
And closer
and closer
and even closer to me.

How my back—
wet and black striped fur clinging to my spine—
shivered.
So many storms I have gathered into me.
And still they came in closer.

THE GRIEVING ROOM
after J.P.

When grief comes
talk to the foxes
curl on the floor
hit eyelids with fists.

Grief is a long dark table
that calls for you to come to it alone.

Thief your heart into pieces.

Make music upon its wood over and over again

banging your hands upon it
until the knuckles bleed and heal and bleed again and again.

The bleeding always comes last.

Grief is a long dark table
that calls for you to come to it alone.

At one end is a skinny man.

There are mountains of food before him
and he keeps and keeps eating.
Before you know it
the food is gone and he still hungers.

Thief your heart into pieces.

Place them on his plate.
He will take the pieces gleefully
blood on his cheeks
chewing loudly.

Stare at him.
Listen to him swallow hard.

When he is done
he will eat the plate.

Start taking apart the table and feed it to him piece by broken piece.
When the table is gone
start peeling back the walls
piling the plaster and wood before him.
Do not separate the nails
place them there as well.
Break the window frames over your knees
sweep the broken glass into his gaping mouth
tear down the beams
and up the floor.
When the room is gone
go to the next room
and then the next one.
Pull the whole house down
to set before the appetite of the skinny man.
Breathe hard
and as if the pile were merely crumbs
watch as he eats it all.

When there is nothing else

nothing but the empty aching world
watching the two of you
and he still stares at you like the rocks below a darkened lighthouse
his eyes

like blue china plates creaking under the strain
like blue faces being held under the cold water

like headlights
ready to swallow everything in its gaze
making the darkness surrounding him even blacker

look around you

your fingers stroking your arms
and wonder what else there is to give.

THE OLD MAN

My heart came back from the wild
with a beard and a broken leg,
a wooden wine cup,
and the footprints of bears on its spine.
It didn't make it to the doorstep.
Instead fell asleep
with the trees looking down
and the wrens
pulling hairs from its beard
to go make their nests with.

THE FEATHER ROOM

I.

Almonds dipped in rose water. Water with orange blossoms. Blossoms the color of peaches. Peaches sliced quietly on white plates. Platters piled with cold plums. The plums are eaten. The eating of light. The chewing of its taste. It catches in the throat. The feathers fill the halls. They glow. They are filled with light bulbs. They are like bulbs in springtime. Knives made of sugar. The soft parts the swans left behind. An eternity of soundless guitars sized for the palm. Soft as water that doesn't spread apart. The inside of the hand to sleep on. Barrels of hair. Barrels of grain. The sand made softer.

A ballroom bricked from clouds. Dresses stitched from ghosts. Fabrics twisting through worlds. Silk. China cabinets. The carpenter is naked with a hammer. Nailing the floor down with figs. He is slowly chewing dates in his mouth and thinking of middle school dances. The gym floor the music moved them across. This is what the room tastes like, fruit and the past. This is what the future is built from. All the fruit you ate. The bowls of grapes eaten after the train ride. The nectarines in your grandmother's living room. The mango twisting under the fork. The mango leaving your fingers sticky. The Japanese plums stolen from the neighbor's overhanging branches. The evidence it dripped on your striped shirts. The summer pulling the shirts off. Juice on your chest drying in the sun. All these things. This is what the walls taste of. Cucumbers sliced and salted. Dill growing in the window. The smell of coffee. Lick the wall. The adding of milk. How the milk moves through the dark liquid, the two becoming something between. The sweetness it left in your mouth. Watermelon seeds spat. Apples cut, apples eaten whole, apples skinned by the grandfathers. Oranges peeled and pulled apart. All the fruit. All the nuts. The almonds, the cashews. The peanut butter cookies in the round tin. The candy hidden on the top shelf. The smell of pralines cooking. Butter and brown sugar melting together. The Persian pastry frying in the pan.

Its stickiness. The way it tastes like roses. Tastes like the honeysuckle. You and your sister picking them from the walls in Southern Louisiana. The way it tastes like jasmine blooming in the nighttime, your mother on the porch in the light of the open door noting its scent moving from under the dark trees and into the house.

II.

It was snowing outside. Walking through it I could see windows glowing in the distance. I could hear the slight sound of a song. It was a chandelier swinging. Somehow the light it cast on the walls reflecting through its costume jewelry made notes. I made my way through the town, walking towards the song.

Outside were ghosts. The city was full of them. Ghosts in long dresses, ghosts in tall hats. The ghosts of mules kicking over buckets of milk. The milk in the air was mistaken for a spirit, and upon hitting the ground the memory of it hanging in space became one. One could see the ghosts moving through the telephone wires, entering into electric sockets and traveling house to house like electricity.

There were ghosts in the garden. Even in the night time, piling dirt and swallowing flowers. The ghost does what it wants, kneels where it is comfortable--pulling a radish, threading a button. At the grandstand a cotillion of ghosts listened to the phonograph, spun photographs all night long. In the haystacks the ghosts sleep, shooting marbles in the barn. In the yards shooting bottle rockets over the fences. Licking the iron of the skillets. Crumbling through the chimneys. Against the photo albums they laugh out loud. In the tall tree behind the church the ghosts of the blue jay gather, a hundred of them calling down to the dead magpie singing in the bushes below.

Everything has a ghost. The measuring cups my mama used. The scissors she held to cut my father's hair. The newspaper on the bathroom floor when she cut ours. The flick of her wrist tossing the curls into the yard for the birds to take. There is a ghost of my sister crying. There is a ghost of the Persian shawl draped over the old trunk in the living room. The shoe store on Oak St. has a ghost as does the memory of going there. My first pocketknife. The three mice I buried. That two of them were yours. Your teeth, your face, the color of your rooms. Everything has a ghost.

The Northwest is a giant of a sleeping ghost. Standing in his palm I trace the softness of his thumbs and think of the squirrels that ran through your chest, the nests in your hair, how dark the winters there are and how the warm winds found us. That warm wind is a trembling ghost that trembles less and less recognizing instead its simple softness. Over the years the ghosts walk up and down the hallway. Sometimes they are loud, sometimes they are nowhere to be seen. The hallway is inside of me. I make piles of sugar in the doorways to see through which rooms the footprints leave tracks.

The snow had covered the city's streets. The ghosts had left many trails. Still trying to head towards the chandelier's song, I got lost following the footprints. I saw a ghost dressed like a policeman and asked if he had maybe seen the ghost of my dead mice. He shook his head and my neck felt wet. Under the transparent brass of his uniform I watched the ghost of his purple heart pump. When he turned away from me, I climbed through an open window to see if any of the kitchens carried my ghosts under their linoleum. I peeled back yellow corners and from beneath the floor poured out water buffalo and grasshopper ghosts. The ghosts of pet gerbils and soap box race-cars. A ghost that looked like France. The ghost of a vase I broke. So many vases I broke. Some were mine, some I had only touched. So many ghosts I made.

I stood by the window and watched the ghosts of presidents and czars placed back to back having duels on the hill. The heads of state walk their paces and turn and shoot. The balls of lead pass through them. The trunks of the trees fill with bullets. Ghosts with hunched backs and sharp spoons come and dig the bullets free to sell them back to the ghosts with guns. When they dig them out, tiny ghosts of bullets escape into the air .

Ghosts die too. I don't know how but under the graveyards there were more graveyards. When a ghost dies the town archer fills the air with flames and the other ghosts cheer. They celebrate the space in their bodies returning to sediment and gravity. They crush the crayfish into wine and drink it until the night peels into the sun.

They celebrate the return to limestone. The return to inertia. Returning to the freckle. The turning back into the body of a widow, the turning into a green floor.

At the bottom of the hill, there is the ghost of a tornado in a house sitting by the fireplace, waiting for its hands to stop blowing out the flames.

Outside the bakery the ghost of a polar bear dips his white paw in red paint.

From the museum a frog ghost has stolen a violin. He has left a lover behind. He uses the music to talk through the worlds to her.

There are children pulling ghosts on string through the snow. The ghost look like keys.

I climbed back out of the window, saw my footprints and continued on opposite of the direction I came from.

III.

The sky was a ballroom
All the planets danced.
There was music behind every wrist,
in every movement.
In every movement we were swans
and our mothers were swans that we came out from.
We were swans
that turned
into bags of arrows,
and we were swans that turned into bags of arrows,
and swans again turning into bags of arrows—
outsmarting bulls and big men,
bringing gold machines into the storms.
Bags of goose blood stitched with feathers—
this is how you trick the constellations.
By drinking them into your dark dark belly.
The dark belly is a closed cabinet of teacups.
A room of teacups trying not to fall.
Rubbing tea leaves across one's skin,
burning oneself to drink it down.

IV.

After stumbling through the snow,
I walk out the city of ghosts and towards the woods,
following the glowing light.
A strange parade makes its way before me.
The foxes walk upright,
wrapped in long black coats.
The coats drag behind them.
The coats cut a wide path through the snow.
The foxes are gods,
the heavens are filled with them.
They come to earth to play cards with the ghosts.
Many dead foxes, many dead ghosts.

The rabbits dress themselves for a party.
They put on their gold teeth, their gold claws,
drape themselves in furs.
They fill their mouths with emeralds and sapphires.
Inside the trees are chandeliers.
The rabbits light the candles and hoist them high.
Through the trunk the glow can be seen for miles.
The hares
the ferrets
the dormice
the moles
the ermine
the badgers
the foxes—
they gather to dance.

In the woods the trees rise like old men.
The old men have rooms like houses.
The rooms are filled with ghosts.
Ghosts of every breath the old men have taken,
every glass they have sipped.

The ghost of every person they have seen sits
in their many living rooms.
This is what death means: to give these ghosts up.
We can only carry them so long,
before they have to taste the world again.
This is how the trees rise:
like the tallest oldest men in all the land,
filled with all the ghosts of all the worlds.
The trees are armoires.
Wardrobes filled with so many ghosts
they burst from the branches,
the leaves growing and falling to the earth.
I have touched so many leaves.
Moved my fingers through them.
Filled my pockets with their fragile bodies.
When they turned to dust,
I moved my body through the dust.
The woods is a dustyard.
A boneyard of no bones.
A ghost yard. A room of vases.

The woods is a room of tree stumps before the future comes.
The future is a long hallway.
It is a bright doorknob on the far end
slowly turning but never opening.
There is something breathing on the other side of the door.
I am in the hallway, always turning.
Peering between the trees,
I watch the animals turn.
They draw me towards them,
their shining palms pulling over my hands.
They robe me in their skin and pour gems down my throat.
We waltz,
we cut squares in the grass.
We link arms, we circle as one.
The woods is an open-face palace.

The sky a ballroom.

The room is so light I pick it up in my hands.
Even with myself so heavy and full of wolf,
standing in the middle,
heavy and choking on rubies,
I can pick it up in my hands.
The sound the night invents
when one walks out of the water surrounds me.
All the animals and all the night they dress themselves inside of
sing:

This is where I saw you.
This is where I see you.
This is where inside of me you sleep.
When I put you into my mouth
it tastes of almonds dipped in rose water.
This is where I taste like this too.

SPRING COMES IN ON THE TAILS

Can you send
the life
we made?
So I put it in a box
and wait for a note to come from her
that will ask this.
Can you send this?
It never does.
I fill the box
take it and dig up a space in the backyard,
put it in there.
Then take it back out and put it on the bookshelf.
Then take it off the bookshelf and put it under the bookshelf.
Then I put the bookshelf in a different room.
I go sit down outside
and for days
listen to a trumpet
playing from far far away.

There is a hole in my chest.
A hole.
Eventually the swallows come,
stuff it
with the straw in their mouths.
They stay all summer long,
then leave.
But here,
I see spring returning
and here they come to me yet again.

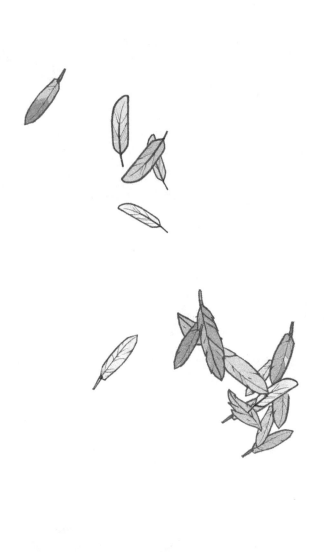

CALL IT MAGIC
CALL IT FISH EYE CALL IT FISH LUNG
CALL YOU MAGIC POCKET OF SCIENCE.

Call you carousel my love.
Call you parasol.
Call you slight rhyme.
Handclap and butter knife collection. Collection bread crumb.
Call you collection back path back to home.
Or morsel soaking up moonlight. Call this something that birds steal,
call this Jazz. Call you collection of Motown. Music stacked. Drum kick
echoed. Hair shined and piled high. High note and heart opening.
Bone split. Knee shaking. Still standing up.
Spitting out those animals those beasts. Collecting their skulls.
Hydra. Harpy. Medea. Jason's heads hung round his hip.
Staining his waist. Bloody belts collected cut and washed. Belt of silver
collected and burnt.

Call you belt of gold. Call you Heracles.
His beautiful body the gods moved themselves through.
Call you however it was that those gods traveled: the belly of a cow.
A swan. A haystack lit on fire. Bowls of fermenting grapes
laid down with slaughtered lambs. Call you how the gods still travel!
Radio light! Spectrum of the magnolia! Newspaper boat.
Fish eye. Fish lung—magic pocket of science!
Smithsonian.
Slow paradise.
Ballroom filled
with slow paradise.
Call you collection of slow paradises moving quickly,
turning on a polished floor in a loose dress
tied tight at the waist—you the music they spin
you their spinning—call you parasol!

Call you carousel! All your horses and all your bears,
going up and down—the zebra tethered
with a bridle of gold and a green feather. All the bees
they watch you. That is all.
They just watch. They have neither fear nor malice for your skin.
They just wish to watch it turn.

FROM THE TOP OF THIS THING

There was a giant thing that had washed up on the beach. Like a whale except bigger. We didn't know if it was alive or dead. We started climbing to the top of it. Parts of it were covered in rock and earth. The rock looked like dragon scales. I picked up a chunk of the scale and launched it into the water. The beast moved.

We could feel it sigh, feel its insides shift. We stepped softer. The wind picked up a little at this height but the sun was still warm.

We reached the top, could see the whole stretch of beach from up there. Could see the whole town. We threw our hands in the air. We had done it! We looked like trophies. We felt like ice cream, like flowers falling. A helicopter flew close and hovered above like a machine from God. The man inside it talked through a loudspeaker. "You did it! You look like trophies! You are ice cream, you are flowers falling! You are flowers grown tall!" He had a bag of confetti. He took fistfuls of the stuff and threw it over us.

Breathless, we sat down for a spell and ate the popsicles we had brought along. They weren't even melted. We shivered a little but in the sunlight our skin felt like it was growing. We stood and started making our way back, the beast breathing under us. In the clay collecting on its hide, you slipped a little. My heart skipped a beat. "Don't fall love, we are not down yet. We are not yet done with this."

SOCK HOP

I was following the little dog through the skinny trees.

I was just collecting water glasses.

I was filling them at the well and carrying them back, one by one.

I was wearing the same shirt as the day before,

and the day before that.

And the day before that.

Asking all my ghosts to join me on the dance floor.

Let's Twist, lets shimmy.

While the room waltzes, I will Watusi.

I was Jimmy Switchblade.

I was the Three Cherries Gang.

I was the tallest cigarette.

I was black jacket black collared collar up, I was actually yellow shirt lost.

I was laying in the dirt and piling it on.

I believed if I kept trying to bury myself

then maybe I could talk to the next world.

I just got dirty.

My belly was heavy.

I could barely move.

For months, I barely moved.

I watched the sun go down and while waiting for it to return,

I slept.

I dreamed of the bicycle but did not know what the bicycle was.

I thought, *What a strange horse that fish is—do I kill it or ride it?*

How do I do either of those?

Instead, I baptized myself with bath water.

I rode the airplanes like they were church,

hoping the chains wouldn't climb this high.

At this altitude all the angels were turning blue.

I stared out the windows

and made a list of my body parts that still worked,

folded it into an envelope,

hoping my mother or a former lover would one day find it.

That list is a poem not a list.

So is this one.

I rode the airplane

until it brought me 530 miles from the room I was born in.

My fists then weren't much smaller than they are now, simply tighter.

I have been shrinking more and more with every month.

The South, it is my beautiful bed.

One day, bury me in it.

Till then, I will touch it from time to time.

Carry me inside its wet wet heat,

I sweat when I walk.

When I walk I see my dreams coming closer.

What I thought was a horse or a fish was really a girl on a bicycle.

She had small fingers but reached them towards me.

I neither killed nor rode her.

All I did was make a hand.

All I did was get wet.

All I did was shake my ribcage like a library in an earthquake.

I spilled books like holy water.

My rooms were a mess.

The ceiling came in closer to read all that I had been—

a thousand years of spines, a white suit stitched from a riverbank.

Bags of the heaviest dust.

I had splinters on my tongue, from licking the cathedral for so long.

I had worked so hard for my sorrow.

So I asked my boss for the night off.

Caught another plane.

Rode it to a dance in Chicago.

I combed my hair, licked down with pomade.

Put my shiniest belt buckle on.

I saw Suzie on the dance floor.

She put a quarter in the jukebox,

grabbed me like a police man, and asked: *What you do Ace?*

I told her I work at a malt shop—sweeping floors, pouring water.

And sometimes I bury things, but I ain't too good at that.

I ain't always too good at that I told her.

She looked at me like we had prayed on the same cliff.

She told me she didn't believe in God anymore.

I told her I still did.

Her and I, we have prayed on the same cliff.

She held me like a handcuff.

I swallowed keys.

I danced with Suzie all night long.

I'm still waiting for the sun to come up.

I don't care if it never does.

I am warm enough.

GOD BLESS NEW YORK IN THE SUNLIGHT. ALL OF ME IS ALL OF YOU AND SO ARE YOU.

Hello.
I think that perhaps I have been here before.
That perhaps I have seen your face before. That perhaps
I know you. There is a field in you.
One that we have both run through. With the sun
bleeding through us. Arms out. Using our bodies
to swallow the wind. Our hearts so full
the birds ate from our hands. Yes.
I know you.
I saw you
on the other side of the tall grass
talking out loud.
I waved to you.
I think perhaps
maybe that
you waved back?
Yes, I think you did.

HE THINKS

She wishes to be his wife. Curling the tips of his mustache he thinks there is magic inside himself. *Those clouds above, are below, inside my roof. Under my fingernails. The universe expands pink gas into purple. The minerals all shiver. This is the same as my atoms. There is magic inside of me.* All of this he marvels at. Curling the mustache even more, he takes the leaves off the trees and melts them with the clocks, walks up the hill, the night at his back, wheelbarrow in his hand, the night in his belly. His skin like a pear's. Tomorrow he will return to mixing his paint, hoping to find the shades of magenta and crimson he has been searching for, to paint what a tiger looks like under a microscope. At lunchtime, he will join her in the kitchen. Sitting at the table they will slice a green apple together. He will marvel even further at how crisp the apple is under his teeth. He will get up and hold his glass under the faucet, filling it to the top. He will marvel the furthest at how smooth he becomes under her eyes, how objects that blue can watch him with so much wonder and he will drink all the water down.

THESE THINGS ARE HOW YOU MAKE ME FEEL:

—a nuclear reactor power plant. Filled not though with any strange harmful energy, only the energy of the sun, daisies, and golden marbles. Filled to the brim. Behind me there is also a rainbow. The reactor that I am, harnesses the power of the rainbow as well.

—a great grey-stoned tall tower that rises out of the ocean. There is nothing around for so far. From the window at the top of the tower I watch the waves, I watch the world. There is nothing but ocean stretching for so far. From here it looks like the biggest thing in the universe—it is the universe. From my room in the tower, sitting above the universe, watching its drops of water move in unison together, I feel like maybe I am bigger.

—I am 17 and running in slow motion through a field lit with light. The dust moves slowly through the air, the sun burning through its tiny bodies. Perhaps it is dust. Perhaps it is magic dust. Perhaps this magical dust is what I am made from. I close my eyes and everything I see floats.

—I am on a boat. It is night. The world has calmed itself simply to hold me inside all that is darkness, simply to rock me gently.

—the subway chambers of Moscow. I am vaulted. I have giant chandeliers hanging from my underground ceilings. I glow with so much light. I am a ballroom for the trains of Russia. If you happen to be a child that has climbed down my steps to enter my body and you yell into it, the echoes will hit those vaulted underground ceilings and bounce. This happens all the time. My dark tunnels are filled with these sounds.

—like I will live forever. Like there is nothing that can harm me. My body will always be young and perfect. There are cities growing inside my chest. The cities look like New York in the fifties. The buildings scrape the clouds. Every automobile is a convertible. The men all wear neckties and hats. The women have beautiful shapes of color on their bodies. Someone has saved a baby, there is a parade. Someone has saved all the babies—there is the biggest parade moving inside of me. The sky explodes with ticker tape. Strangers are kissing in the streets. Their kisses are what make me live forever.

—like honey and trombones. Like honey and trombones.

THEY WERE IN BED
UNDER THE CEILING LIGHT,
HE WAS DRAWING CIRCUS ANIMALS
SHE WAS READING ABOUT DEBUTANTES

I told her
Our love is our heads
placed inside the mouth of a lion
but the lion would not ever lion-bite down.
His breath is hot. We can feel it over our ears
but lion wont lion-bite down.
She responds by saying So
you are saying
we can get a baby bear?
I say
No.
Maybe a baby lion.
But the lion would be so sad
and dream of Africa she says.
What would the bear dream of then I ask.
Trees I guess. And napping.
Hmmmm I say.
She answers this non-commitment with But bears are so cute.
He could sleep in our bed.
He could sleep in our bed until he ate it, I point out.
She sighs,
turns a page in her book
and head down, says I still love you.
I can see there is something about a Russian ballroom
on the page she is reading
She asks What will you dream about tonight?
The Mediterranean I answer.

You?
Telephone poles she says. And bright blue houses
on Irish cliffs.
That's pretty I tell her.
The lion, our heads still somehow both fitting in its mouth,
manages to purr.
My whole body is warm.
My whole body is something that happens
when the trapeze becomes just a chandelier watching.

FRUIT

I loved a girl who moved to Antarctica.
She writes me sometimes.
She tells me about the naked beasts that are there
and the orchards that grow under the snow,
how the fruit tastes sweeter after digging it out of ice.
Her hands freeze from the digging
but the fruit tastes sweeter.
She writes,
Did you know
there is a fish here called the Ice Fish? They don't have any red blood
so nothing to carry the oxygen around.
They have clear blood and you can see right through their scales.
At the start of winter, Antarctica's ice expands
40,000 square miles a day—did you know that?
Did you know there is an active volcano here?
And that there is a breed of small white snow deer
that bury themselves in the banks at the volcano's base,
and in the morning, crow to the light?
I would like to keep one here with me.
The red igloo she sleeps in
is shared with three others.
They sleep in bunks.
The inside walls are of old polished wood she tells me,
like her grandfather's house in San Francisco.
She keeps a plant in the kitchen
and drinks cups of tea all day long,
writing by the small window.
The penguins here play a game similar to bowling
where a bunch of them stand in a group
and one of them slides down the hill at the others
to see how many he can knock over.

This is very very funny to watch.
She likes it there all right.
There are many times though, when she is lonely.
She says there is a part of her
that claws in how heavy alone she at times becomes.
I am lonely sometimes.
It's like an ocean of black oil
and the part of me that is all that I was before
is a white stone
sinking slowly in the ocean.
I don't really know what I am anymore.
What am I doing?
I miss the afternoon.
It is only ever morning or night here.
There are evenings when the beasts howl so much
that the loneliness goes away.
But other nights where the howls only cause her to sink more.
She misses her animals back home.
She writes lists,
lists of anything—
the names of past pets.
The places she wants to see before she dies.
All the streets she has lived on.
She stays up late
smoking cigarettes,
writing letters to nobody.
The ones she sends to me
I keep inside a fireproof box.
I mail gloves and scarves to her,
hold blankets like horses,
and board planes for clear water.

ALONG THE SANDY

There were two trips we made together to the river. The first one with everyone else, you in your new second-hand swimsuit that fit loosely. Aaron threw mud on your back. On the following trip I swallowed water offshore. I thought I would drown and you tried to help me. No matter the weight of the day or the lightness of the night, my body holds these trips. Along with the crest of the Northwest, the mountains of its giants and its trees—the life it gave me is carried by my body. I am thankful for how the dark hands of Oregon held us. That the bees in my chest finally slept soundly. That fruit grew. That fruit was picked by us from both our bodies. Held up in the sunlight. Turned over in our hands with wonder and then shared with each other. This fruit was shared. The juice from it is not a stain, just something that fell. We put our hands over our eyes to keep from going blind, we put the china of our limbs into the current. Porcelain, smooth, curving. What plates we polished off. The ones you left me with are very pretty. Such golden light the rivers in my country hold.

They speak well of you.

LIKE A PIANO IN A HOUSE ON A CLIFF

You came into my house.
You picked the lock.
And while I was gone you crept in.
You were wearing black socks a black mask and moved
like a cat dancing silently alone.
You knew which rooms to go through
which steps to step over
took the shining stones from out of the bedroom's drawers
found the lock behind the painting in the study
knew the combination
pulled out the bills
the pearls
the wedding ring of a grandmother from the bottom of a sock
the grandfather's watch of gold
hidden under the refrigerator.
You used my toothbrush.
Put it back upside down.
Emptied the can of shaving cream into the dog bowl.
Put the eggs in the meat drawer
the meat into the washing machine
and the wet clothes
you took and cut into strips
laid them inside the silverware drawer
used my costumes to cut your dinner.
After eating your fill on the yard's tulips
you sat yourself on the leather couch in the living room.
Read all my letters.
Took off all your clothes.
Let your burglar wear fall
like night from the sun's shoulders.
Draped yourself in jewelry.

Let the secrets of your body trade secrets with my treasures.
Pushing your toes into the thick carpet
your calves tightened
muscles thick as safari thunder.
You read my letters again
spoke the sentences out loud
and naked but for strings and strings of pearls
the weight of emeralds on your breasts
your skin licking all the soft silver of my home.
You filled the halls with your voice
curling my words like my hand were there to move through you.
All of this is true.
All of this is *exactly* how it happened
All of this is true
except for the part of you breaking in.
When you came into me
like a white flower to a little bit of water
I left the door wide open for you to step through.

ALEXIS

The simpleness of the wrist.
A fountain in the ground.
The catching of birds.
Laying their collected feathers side by side on the kitchen floor
until the tiles were filled.
In the afternoon light
we let the birds go—
all of them—
but they stayed,
content to sit on the porch
watching while we filled the pillowcases.

WHAT HIS FATHER SAID

"My heart was a bathtub.
I filled it with so much water.
So much warm water.
I sat in it.
It was so warm.
When it got cold I turned the water back on.
The water flowed over the sides. I kept filling it.
The water covered the bathroom floor.
The water went under the door and down the hall.
The water filled the hall.
I was sitting in it the whole time.
It was so warm.
The water filled the whole house.
Poured out of the windows on the second floor.
It flooded the attic.
I was still sitting in it.
It felt so good on my body.
Our lawn became a swimming pool.
The street a creek.
Downtown became a lake.
City Hall a lake house.
Your grandfather started going to work in a rowboat.
I saw the mayor in a canoe.
For some reason, the mayor had feathers in his mouth.
I saw him from the bathroom's window.
When he paddled past, he smiled at me.
I was in the tub the whole time.
It was so warm.
So warm.
I flooded the whole town.
That's why we moved here."

THIS IS WHAT THE SCORPIONS BRING

The tomatoes were so fat.
We grew them that way.

Inside your arms I grew to love their taste. There were so many of them we had to throw some away. They filled our steps. So red and so plump. You fed them to me with basil. Afterwards, I would hold the plates under the hot water and stare out the window, watching Sweetbelly climbing in the trees, her dusty hair singing loudly in the dusk. The desert fell out behind the branches, our daughter moving in the disappearing light, like something the scorpions would flock in awe towards.

I called out to you, Where is Stickylove? You called back, said he was right here, at your feet, turning the pages in a magazine, holding a song in his mouth, making it up as he did. You asked me to bring you a piece of cornbread with the jar of fig jam we had made. I washed off a knife, cut a square from the center of the pan, and put it on a clean saucer.

WITH THE HENS OUTSIDE

The man on the record player sings
We are not afraid to die.
And with the spinach pulled from outside
being washed between my hands
and the water sizzling in the iron skillet
cleaning the skillet the way you taught me how
and the chicken in the fridge
and a tomato to cut
and corn to clean
and apples to bake
and brown sugar and butter and chocolate
with ceiling fans worshipping my skin
with you and your bicycle
on your way home
with the mint freshly picked from the garden
still scenting my fingers
and being so incredibly unafraid
to look you in your eyes
with the gentle beauty of not knowing
I am inclined to believe him.

WHAT HE SAID

I told her
simply
that
I feel like a field again.

KOOKUBURA

Stumbling through the pasture, the grass is a small piano a long piano a soft hand twirling piano. The night is a storefront based on trade—it gives one the pieces of itself for pieces of oneself. The tree stumps are for sitting. The silver in the sky for polishing. The forest is a collection of whistles waiting to be whittled. My elbows, bone smoothed into plates. I am leaving them on the doorstep. I have knocked on the heavy dark wood and run to a nearby bush. Footsteps announce the door opening. He takes the food. He hungers. He makes the birds call simply by looking. He hungers. I want to feed. My face is a sometimes rifle. A sometimes screaming child. But in some lakes, I reflect a harp. A great big bowl. And a pair of giving hands. All I wish is to feed.

I woke up light. Light as a pencil and ready to sing. I called my mother to tell her this. She was happy as a song. The guns are in the ground. You can't even see the triggers. I can't even see the shovel. I hear fires from somewhere, burning, but I can't even smell the smoke. I am behind the bush, watching from the leaves. Some of them are in my pocket turning colors. He knows I'm here. He slowly eats what I have made. He whistles. He whistles again. I know the whistle is my name. I know there is alligator in my heart. My heart is made up of vertebrae. Antelope in my heart. Kookubura in my heart. My heart is a gum tree. My heart is Africa. My heart is a still river made of gold water and mud.

He finishes the food I have brought. He eats all that I filled the plates with. He looks in my direction. I am still hidden by my leaves. He knows I am here. He smiles. He has less teeth than I would have thought. He cleans the elbows that are now plates and sets them down. He leaves a flower on each one. The flowers are not roses. They are too beautiful. He goes inside. My heart is round. My heart is bowl. I place the flowers in it. I never hear the door lock. I sit under the doorknob, feeling warm. I watch the dark trade places with the stars and wait for the bells to ring. My heart is patient. My heart is boxing ring emptied. Bird cage nesting. Orchard dirt running. Nothing can hurt me. I love you fearlessly. I have your heart. I do not know what size the spoons made from my history books are but you told me, *You have my heart*. Your heart is convex. Your heart is Galileo. I am dancing in the middle of the road. No car can touch me, I am making telescopes. I am feathers pulled but growing back. Nothing can hurt me. The loudest bird in America is asleep.

ABOUT THE AUTHOR

Anis Mojgani is Black and Iranian. He is the author of *Over the Anvil We Stretch* (2008), as well as a National and International Poetry Slam Champion. His work has appeared on HBO, NPR, as well as in journals *RATTLE* and *The Legendary*. Originally from New Orleans, Anis has called Portland, OR home for six years but will soon be a Texan. This is his second book.

ACKNOWLEDGMENTS

The poems "The bicycle room" and "One Saturday afternoon before I was born" first appeared in the *The Legendary* literary journal.

The poem "Beehive/Lodestone" is directly inspired by lines from the song "Bloodbuzz Ohio" written by Matt Berninger of The National.

The poem "Won't you come out tonight" takes its title from the song "Buffalo Gals."

Elements of the poem "This is what the scorpions bring" are taken from a piece by A. Davis.

There are many places scattered around the country that have held me: some of them couches, some of them apartments, some castles built inside of others. O how I love so many of you. I am eternally grateful to have you people in my life. There are many rooms inside of me, whose walls are shared by yours.

To the Write Bloody Family: it is an honor to be a part of this press with people like you. To its editors (and to Jeff McDaniel) for their assistance with the manuscript, thank you very very very much for your thoughts and suggestions in helping shape this joker. As well as a hearty thank you to Sarah Kay and Lea Deschenes for their assistance in getting this to press. A particular thank you to Cristin for her tireless support in this crazy community of ours, I cannot thank you enough for your wisdom and knowledge and the selflessness with which you share it. And of course thank you so much to Derrick and his continuous efforts to push Write Bloody up the mountain, there is much steepness, and in spite of the climb and the tiredness you keep pushing on. Thank you.

To Houses: Pointy, Hippie, Cowboy, Pillsbury, Ted, and Wagner, and the family that has stretched between them over the years since Savannah, thank you for being home. Your faces always will be.

Thank you Mom & Pop, Shokufeh, Naysan, Sam, and Kalani, and all my family for continuously being there for me even when I retreat into the cave of creating.

And to Alexis: fearlessly. Fearlessly, fearlessly, fearlessly.

NEW WRITE BLOODY BOOKS FOR 2011

DEAR FUTURE BOYFRIEND
A Write Bloody reissue of Cristin O'Keefe Aptowicz's first book of poetry

HOT TEEN SLUT
A Write Bloody reissue of Cristin O'Keefe Aptowicz's second book of poetry
about her time writing for porn

WORKING CLASS REPRESENT
A Write Bloody reissue of Cristin O'Keefe Aptowicz's third book of poetry

OH, TERRIBLE YOUTH
A Write Bloody reissue of Cristin O'Keefe Aptowicz's fourth book of poetry
about her terrible youth

38 BAR BLUES
A collection of poems by C.R .Avery

WORKIN' MIME TO FIVE
Humor by Derrick Brown

REASONS TO LEAVE THE SLAUGHTER
New poems by Ben Clark

YESTERDAY WON'T GOODBYE
New poems by Brian Ellis

WRITE ABOUT AN EMPTY BIRDCAGE
New poems by Elaina M. Ellis

THESE ARE THE BREAKS
New prose by Idris Goodwin

BRING DOWN THE CHANDELIERS
New poems by Tara Hardy

THE FEATHER ROOM
New poems by Anis Mojgani

LOVE IN A TIME OF ROBOT APOCALYPSE
New poems by David Perez

THE NEW CLEAN
New poems by Jon Sands

THE UNDISPUTED GREATEST WRITER OF ALL TIME
New poems by Beau Sia

SUNSET AT THE TEMPLE OF OLIVES
New poems by Paul Suntup

GENTLEMAN PRACTICE
New poems by Buddy Wakefield

HOW TO SEDUCE A WHITE BOY IN TEN EASY STEPS
New poems by Laura Yes Yes

OTHER WRITE BLOODY BOOKS (2003 - 2010)

STEVE ABEE, GREAT BALLS OF FLOWERS (2009)
New poems by Steve Abee

EVERYTHING IS EVERYTHING (2010)
New poems by Cristin O'Keefe Aptowicz

CATACOMB CONFETTI (2010)
New poems by Josh Boyd

BORN IN THE YEAR OF THE BUTTERFLY KNIFE (2004)
Poetry collection, 1994-2004 by Derrick Brown

I LOVE YOU IS BACK (2006)
Poetry compilation (2004-2006) by Derrick Brown

SCANDALABRA (2009)
New poetry compilation by Derrick Brown

DON'T SMELL THE FLOSS (2009)
New Short Fiction Pieces By Matty Byloos

THE BONES BELOW (2010)
New poems by Sierra DeMulder

THE CONSTANT VELOCITY OF TRAINS (2008)
New poems by Lea C. Deschenes

HEAVY LEAD BIRDSONG (2008)
New poems by Ryler Dustin

UNCONTROLLED EXPERIMENTS IN FREEDOM (2008)
New poems by Brian Ellis

CEREMONY FOR THE CHOKING GHOST (2010)
New poems by Karen Finneyfrock

POLE DANCING TO GOSPEL HYMNS (2008)
Poems by Andrea Gibson

CITY OF INSOMNIA (2008)
New poems by Victor D. Infante

THE LAST TIME AS WE ARE (2009)
New poems by Taylor Mali

IN SEARCH OF MIDNIGHT: THE MIKE MCGEE HANDBOOK OF AWESOME (2009)
New poems by Mike McGee

OVER THE ANVIL WE STRETCH (2008)
New poems by Anis Mojgani

ANIMAL BALLISTICS (2009)
New poems by Sarah Morgan

NO MORE POEMS ABOUT THE MOON (2008)
NON-Moon poems by Michael Roberts

MILES OF HALLELUJAH (2010)
New poems by Rob "Ratpack Slim" Sturma

SPIKING THE SUCKER PUNCH (2009)
New poems by Robbie Q. Telfer

RACING HUMMINGBIRDS (2010)
New poems by Jeanann Verlee

LIVE FOR A LIVING (2007)
New poems by Buddy Wakefield

WRITE BLOODY ANTHOLOGIES

THE ELEPHANT ENGINE HIGH DIVE REVIVAL (2009)
Poetry by Buddy Wakefield, Derrick Brown,
Anis Mojgani, Shira Erlichman and many more!

THE GOOD THINGS ABOUT AMERICA (2009)
An illustrated, un-cynical look at our American Landscape. Various authors.
Edited by Kevin Staniec and Derrick Brown

JUNKYARD GHOST REVIVAL (2008)
Poetry by Andrea Gibson, Buddy Wakefield, Anis Mojgani,
Derrick Brown, Robbie Q, Sonya Renee and Cristin O'Keefe Aptowicz

THE LAST AMERICAN VALENTINE:
ILLUSTRATED POEMS TO SEDUCE AND DESTROY (2008)
24 authors, 12 illustrators team up for a collection of non-sappy love poetry.
Edited by Derrick Brown

LEARN THEN BURN (2010)
Anthology of poems for the classroom. Edited by Tim Stafford and Derrick Brown.

LEARN THEN BURN TEACHER'S MANUAL (2010)
Companion volume to the *Learn Then Burn* anthology. Includes lesson plans and worksheets for educators.
Edited by Tim Stafford and Molly Meacham.

WRITEBLOODY
QUALITY AMERICAN BOOKS

WWW.WRITEBLOODY.COM

WRITEBLOODY
QUALITY AMERICAN BOOKS

PULL YOUR BOOKS UP BY THEIR BOOTSTRAPS

Write Bloody Publishing distributes and promotes great books of fiction, poetry and art every year. We are an independent press dedicated to quality literature and book design, with an office in Long Beach, CA.

Our employees are authors and artists so we call ourselves a family. Our design team comes from all over America: modern painters, photographers and rock album designers create book covers we're proud to be judged by.

We publish and promote 8-12 tour-savvy authors per year. We are grass-roots, D.I.Y., bootstrap believers. Pull up a good book and join the family. Support independent authors, artists and presses.

Visit us online:
WRITEBLOODY.COM

CPSIA information can be obtained
at www.ICGtesting.com
Printed in the USA
FSHW010404270821
84277FS